# The Secret Travels
# of Koala Bears

# About Wise & Wide

- A systematic 6-level English reading program based on Lexile® measures
- Diverse and interesting topics chosen from the elementary curriculums of Korea and English speaking western countries
- Well-written books in various forms including fiction stories, descriptive texts, and classics retold
- The informative but original fiction stories grab your interest, leading to the easy and clear understanding of the educational content.
- Improve thinking skills with solid after-reading activities at all levels of the series.

**Wise & Wide** is a 6-level English reading program that consists of 60 books and each level is systematically divided by Lexile® measures. The Lexile® Framework for Reading is the most popular reading measuring system in American formal education curriculums and many English programs. Over 20 out of 50 states in the U.S. mark Lexile® measures directly on students' final report cards and over 300 well-known publishers adopt and use Lexile® measures.

Experience many kinds of readings written by professional writers from the U.S. and England. They used interesting topics that were carefully chosen after analyzing elementary curriculums from around the world including Korea, the U.S., England, and Australia among many others. Comprehensive after-reading activities including graphic organizers, speaking tasks, and After-reading Tests are ready for you.

## Levels in the series and their corresponding Lexile® measures

| Level | Lexile® measures | U.S. Grade |
| --- | --- | --- |
| Level 1 | Below 200L | Pre K - K |
| Level 2 | 190L - 400L | Lower Grade 1 |
| Level 3 | 350L - 530L | Upper Grade 1 |
| Level 4 | 420L - 650L | Grade 2 |
| Level 5 | 520L - 940L | Grade 3 - 4 |
| Level 6 | 830L - 1070L | Grade 5 - 6 |

* Smart Readers: Wise & Wide level 1 is applicable to the preschool level in the U.S.
* The source of the relationship between Lexile® measures and U.S. school grades: CCSS(Common Core State Standards) FOR ENGLISH LANGUAGE ARTS, APPENDIX A (2012, which is used by 45 states in the U.S.)

# Topic List

| | Level 1 | Level 2 | Level 3 | Level 4 | Level 5 | Level 6 |
|---|---|---|---|---|---|---|
| Book 1 | Science>Biology: The hibernation of animals<br>Story | Science>Biology: Living and nonliving things<br>Story | Science>Biology> Animals & the Environment: Sea otters<br>Story | Environment> Living with nature: The diver & the persimmon tree<br>Story | Science>Biology> Animal: Amazing animals of the Amazon<br>Story | Science>Biology: Germs, transmitted diseases<br>Story |
| Book 2 | Literature> World classics: Aesop's fables<br>Story | Literature> Traditional fairy tale: Old tales about stones<br>Story | Social Studies> Economy: To run a business to make and save money<br>Story | Science>Biology> Plants: Photosynthesis<br>Story | Science>Earth science: Earth's layers, earthquakes, volcanoes, and earth's atmosphere<br>Report | Mathematics> Sequence: The golden ratio & the Fibonacci sequence<br>Story |
| Book 3 | Science>Physics: How shadows are formed<br>Story | Literature> World classics: Peter Pan<br>Story | Science>Scientific technology: Nanobots<br>Story | Literature>Myths: World's creation stories<br>Story | Literature> Legend: The story of King Arthur<br>Story | Literature>Myths: Constellation myths<br>Story |
| Book 4 | Literature> Traditional literature: The Talmud<br>Story | Science>Biology> Animal: Polar bears<br>Story | Science>Biology> Animal: Mountain gorillas<br>Story | Social Studies> Cultural anthropology: Amazing ancient cultures of the world<br>Story | Science> Earth science: Clouds and weather<br>Story | Literature> Human & animals: The friendship between a girl and a horse<br>Story |
| Book 5 | Social Studies> Ethics: Rules in daily life<br>Story | Science>Biology: The five senses<br>Report | Social Studies> Cultural anthropology: Astonishing festivals<br>Report | Art>Music: Stories from two operas<br>Story | Social Studies> World culture & history: The Renaissance<br>Story | |
| Book 6 | Social Studies> World geography & travel: Tourist attractions around the world<br>Story | Science>Biology> Animal: Dinosaurs<br>Story | Science> Astronomy: The solar system<br>Story | Social Studies> People: Three great people who overcame hardships<br>Story | Science>Scientific technology: The wonderful world of robots<br>Report | |
| Book 7 | | Social Studies> Cultural anthropology: Mythological monsters from around the world<br>Report | | Science & Social Studies> Technology & culture: Inventions from around the world<br>Report | Art>Works of art: Famous paintings<br>Report | |
| Book 8 | | | | Social Studies> History: the California Gold Rush<br>Report | Social Studies & Science> Psychology: Psychology in everyday life<br>Story | |
| Book 9 | | | | | | |
| Book 10 | | | | | | |

* 10 books in each level will be published.

# How to Use This Book

### •Before Reading

You can easily find the topic and what kind of story you are about to read.

### •The text

All the stories were written by professional writers from the U.S. and England, so you will read authentic and appropriate English sentences and expressions in every book in the series.

### •Pop Quiz

Check out right away if you understand what you have just read by solving a pop quiz that checks your comprehension.

### •Key Words

The key words and expressions on each page are listed for you to easily study them.

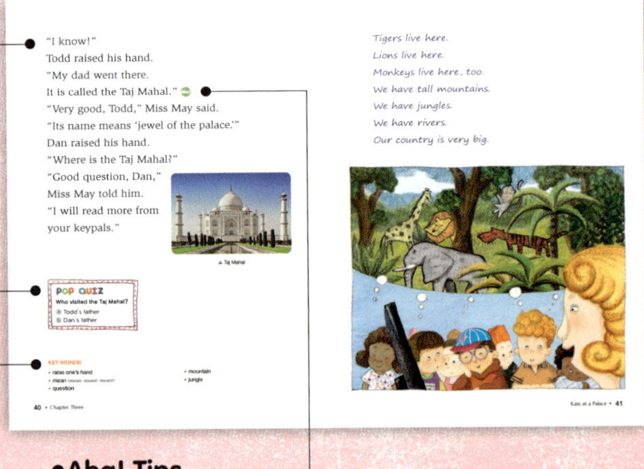

### •Aha! Tips

Download free Korean explanations at *www.ihappyhouse.co.kr* for all of the sentences marked with "Aha!". These explain cultural, scientific, and economic knowledge or they deal with aspects of English such as grammatical structures or idiomatic expressions. There are lots of "Aha! Tips" to help you understand the text.

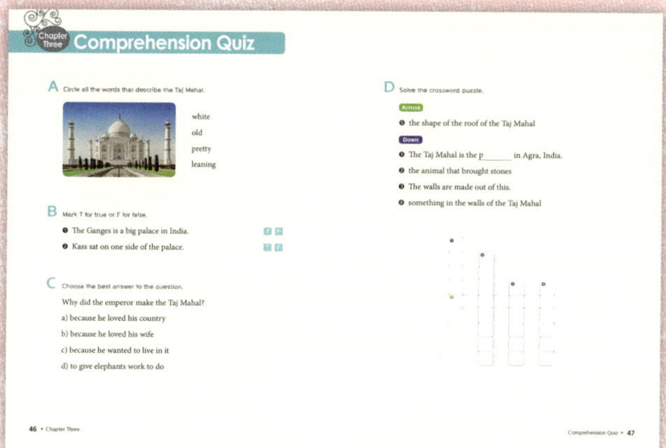

### •Comprehension Quiz

After reading one chapter, solve various questions to find out if you fully understand the content.

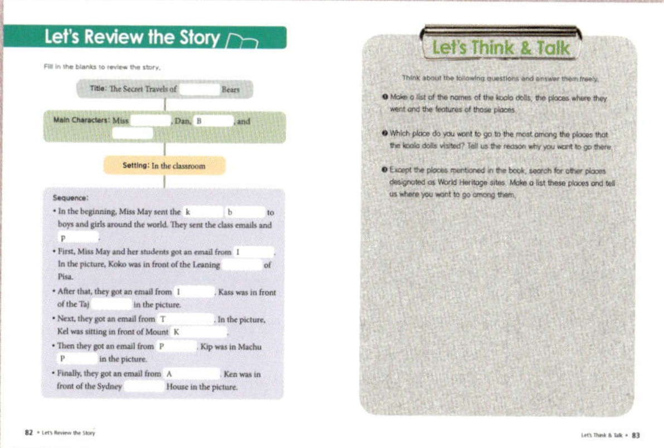

### •Let's Review the Story /
### •Let's Think & Talk

Fill in the blanks in the organizer to summarize the whole story. Express your own thinking and feelings about the story by answering the questions. You can build up logic and reasoning skills for your essay examinations in the future.

## Appendix

### Audio CD
In the CD audio book form, the texts are read vividly by American professional voice actors.

### After-reading Test
Solve an additionally provided After-reading Test for each book.

### The Korean translation, Answer Keys, a Word Quiz, a Word List, and Aha! Tips for each book
You can download them for free at *www.ihappyhouse.co.kr*

# Before Reading

## The Secret Travels of Koala Bears



Level 1-6,
Lexile® 190L

•Social Studies〉World geography & travel
•Story

## Meet World Heritage!

Among all the cultural assets and wonders of nature all around the world, we consider that some of them deserve the protection and preservation of mankind, so we designate them as "World Heritage" to protect them. These sites are designated as "World Heritage" by UNESCO. UNESCO is short for the United Nations Educational, Scientific and Cultural Organization.

Included among these are natural heritage sites, cultural heritage sites, and combined heritage sites that mix cultural and natural factors together. Natural heritage sites are places that have a natural environment with great value or animals and plants which need to be protected. For example, there is Iguazu National Park in Brazil. Cultural heritage includes buildings, ruins, sculptures, paintings, etc. For example, there is the Leaning Tower of Pisa in Italy. Machu Picchu in Peru is a good example of a combined heritage site.

In the book, let's check out World Heritage sites that represent each continent.

## Summary

Miss May class has five koala dolls which represent the class. One day, Miss May tells her class an interesting plan. It is to send the five koala dolls all over the world. But where she will send them is a secret. If friends from the countries where the dolls visit send pictures and emails, her students will find clues in the emails and pictures and guess where the koala dolls are. In addition, they will learn about special buildings or places there. Her students think Miss May's plan is interesting, so they decorate the koala dolls beautifully and get ready to send them to countries around the world. What countries will the koala dolls visit? Let's follow them together.

# Contents

# The Secret Travels of Koala Bears

# The Secret Travels
of Koala Bears

# The Keypal Plan

Miss May had class toys.

She had five koala bears at school.

It was a Monday.

Miss May clapped her hands.

"Class!"

"Yes," the children said.

"I have a fun idea.

Let us send the koalas far away.

They will visit other countries." Aha!

### KEY WORDS

- keypal
- plan
- class
- koala (bear)
- Monday
- clap one's hands
- have an idea (have-had-had)

- fun
- let us + *Verb*
- send (send-sent-sent)
- far away
- visit
- other
- country

Koko
Kip
Kass
Kel
Ken

Miss May patted a toy koala.

"They will go around the world.

We will learn about the countries."

"Will they go to England?" asked Beth.

"Will they go to France?"

Todd pointed to a map.

"Will they go to Spain?" asked Dan.

Miss May put a finger on her lips.

"It is a secret."

**KEY WORDS**

- pat
- go around the world (go-went-gone)
- learn
- England
- ask
- France
- point to
- map
- Spain
- put a finger on one's lips (put-put-put)
- secret

"Will you give us clues?" asked Beth.

"You will have clues," Miss May said.

"Our keypals will send emails."

"What are keypals?" Dan asked.

"Keypals are boys and girls.

They live in other countries.

They will send us emails.

They will send pictures," Miss May answered.

Beth smiled.

"Our keypals will be our friends."

"Yes, they will," Miss May said.

"The pictures and emails will give us clues.

I call this our Keypal Plan.

Todd, here is Koko.

Here is Kip."

**KEY WORDS**

- **give** (give-gave-given)
- **clue**
- **email**

- **live in**
- **picture**
- **answer**

- **smile**
- **call**
- **here +** *be Verb*

koko
LiP
B
33

Todd gave Koko a red tie.

He put a green tie on Kip.

"Beth, here is Kass.

Here is Kel."

Beth put a blue bow on Kass.

She gave Kel a pink bow.

▲ bow

"Dan, here is Ken."

Dan put a yellow tie on Ken.

Each koala had a pouch.

The pouch was on its tummy.

The children put things in the pouches.

The first thing was a school picture.

The next thing was some candy.

Last, they put in a letter.

This is what it said.

### POP QUIZ

What three things are in the koalas' pouches?

ⓐ a picture, a toy, and money
ⓑ a picture, candy, and a letter

**KEY WORDS**

- tie
- bow
- each
- pouch
- tummy
- first
- next
- some
- candy
- last
- letter

Dear keypals, **Aha!**

Here is a gift from our class.

It is a toy koala.

Look in its pouch.

You will find candy.

You will find a picture.

Please send us an email.

Please send us pictures.

Tell us about your country.

We will guess where you live.

Thanks,

Your keypals in the U.S.A.

**KEY WORDS**

- dear
- gift
- **find** (find-found-found)
- please
- guess
- where
- thanks

The children waved to the bears.

"Bye, bye! Have a fun trip!"

Miss May put the bears in boxes.

She went to the post office.

She sent the koalas different places.

She kept each place a secret.

# Comprehension Quiz

**A** Match the color of tie with each koala bear.

❶ Koko ·

❷ Kip ·

❸ Kass ·

❹ Kel ·

❺ Ken ·

· a) yellow 

· b) red 

· c) blue 

· d) green 

· e) pink 

**B** Mark T for true or F for false.

❶ Miss May has real koala bears in class.   T   F

❷ A koala bear's pouch is on its tummy.   T   F

❸ Miss May put six koala bears in boxes.   T   F

❹ The bears will go around the world.   T   F

C Choose the best answer to each question.

**❶** Why does Miss May want to send the koala bears to countries around the world?

a) She does not like the koala bears.

b) She wants to teach her class about the world.

c) She wants to share the koala bears.

d) She is taking a trip and wants to bring the koala bears with her.

**❷** What was the first thing the boys and the girls put in the koalas' pouches?

a) candy                          b) a bow

c) a letter                       d) a school picture

**❸** Where will the boys and the girls find clues about the countries their keypals are in?

a) in the pictures and emails

b) in a box

c) in a video

d) in the pouches of the koala bears

# Where Did Koko Go?

It was another Monday.

Miss May clapped her hands.

"Boys and girls, I have a picture for you."

She tapped the computer.

The smart board showed a building.

"Can you turn the picture?"

Beth tipped her head to the side.

"The building is leaning."

▲ smart board

**KEY WORDS**

- another
- tap
- smart board
- show
- building

- can + *Verb*
- turn
- tip
- to the side
- leaning

- That's right.
- tower
- too
- everyone

"That's right."

Miss May smiled.

"This tower leans to the side."

"Wow," Todd tipped his head, too.

"It is a leaning tower."

Everyone tipped their heads to the side.

"There is Koko with his red tie." Aha!

Miss May pointed to him.

"He is in front of the tower."

Koko had a flag.

It was tied to his paw.

It was green, white, and red.

It looked like Koko was waving the flag.

Dan waved at the picture.

Miss May read the email.



Miss May pointed to the tower.
"This is a bell tower.
It is part of a church.
It has seven bells.
The bells can play a song."

**KEY WORDS**

- in front of
- flag
- be tied to
- paw
- look like
- **read** (read-read-read)

- **know** (know-knew-known)
- bell
- part of
- church
- play a song

"Why does the tower lean?" Dan asked.

"The ground on one side is soft," Miss May told him.

"The tower is heavy. It is so heavy it leans."

"Will it fall over?" Beth asked.

"No. People worked to fix it."

Miss May read more of the email.

The tower is 183 feet tall.
That is about 56 meters.
You can go up the tower.
It has 297 steps.



- ground
- soft
- heavy
- fall over (fall-fell-fallen)
- work
- fix

- more
- feet
- meter (1 m = 100 cm)
- go up
- step

"May I go to the tower?

May I ring the bells?" Beth asked.

"Me, too!" Dan and Todd said.

Miss May smiled.

"Your keypals told us more."

▲ Italy shaped like a boot

We like to play soccer.
We like to eat pasta. Aha!
Our country is the shape
of a boot.

▲ pasta



**KEY WORDS**

- **may**
- **ring** (ring-rang-rung)
- **play soccer**
- **eat** (eat-ate-eaten)

- **pasta**
- **shape**
- **boot**

"Is Koko in Italy?" Todd said.

"The flag of Italy is green, white, and red."

Beth looked at the map.

"Italy is shaped like a boot."

"I know!" Dan jumped up.

"My father went to Italy.

He gave me a present.

It was a toy Leaning Tower of Pisa."

"Very good, children.

You are right," Miss May said.

She read the rest of the email.

▲ Leaning Tower of Pisa

This is the Leaning
Tower of Pisa.
We live in the town of
Pisa, Italy.

Ciao!
Your keypals in Italy

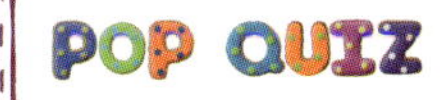


**What present did Dan get from Dad?**

ⓐ the flag of Italy
ⓑ a toy Leaning Tower of Pisa

**KEY WORDS**

- jump up
- present (= gift)
- rest

- town
- ciao

# Comprehension Quiz

**A** Mark T for true or F for false.

❶ The bells of the tower can play a song.  T  F

❷ Beth's father went to Italy.  T  F

❸ Koko was on the top of the tower.  T  F

**B** Choose the best answer to each question.

❶ Why does the Leaning Tower of Pisa lean?

a) It was built that way.

b) It is broken.

c) It is heavy and the ground is soft.

d) It has too many things in it.

❷ Why will the Leaning Tower of Pisa not fall down?

a) The ground is hard now.

b) People worked to fix it.

c) People tore it down.

d) It is not tall enough to fall.

**C** Solve the crossword puzzle.



❶ The leaning tower is in __________.

❺ The tower is part of a __________.

❻ The keypals from Italy like to eat __________.

❼ There are seven __________ in the tower.



❷ The children in Italy like to play __________.

❸ The tower has 297 __________.

❹ Italy is the shape of a __________.

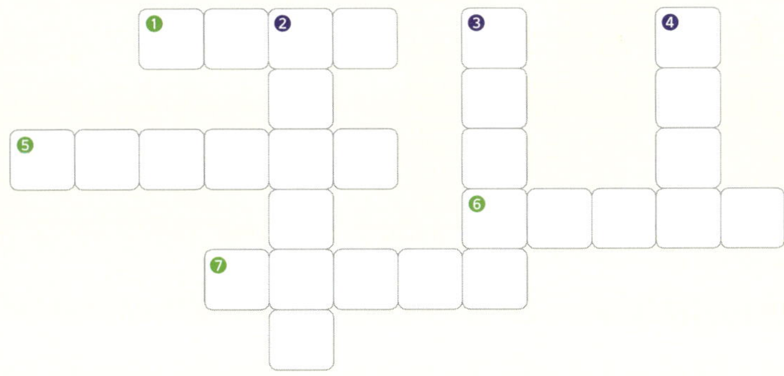

# Kass at a Palace

It was Tuesday morning.

Miss May said, "Boys and girls.

I have some news."

She took out her phone.

"We have an email from our keypals.

They sent a picture."

She put her phone by the computer.

She tapped a button.

A picture showed on the smart board.

Miss May read the email.



- palace
- Tuesday
- news
- take out (take-took-taken)
- by
- button

Dear keypals,

Thank you for sending Kass.
She is happy in our class.
We live in a hot place.
The name of our country starts with a vowel. **Aha!**
Our country has a big river.
It is called the Ganges. **Aha!**
Do you know where we live?

▼ the Ganges

The children looked at the picture.

Kass sat on a bench.

She wore the blue bow.

She was in front of a pretty palace.



- start with
- vowel
- river
- be called
- the Ganges

- sit (sit-sat-sat)
- bench
- wear (wear-wore-worn)
- pretty

The palace had a long pool.

The pool was shiny.

Trees and grass grew by the pool.

Towers were by the pool.

The top of the palace looked like a cupcake.

"Where is that?" asked Beth.

"Listen for the clues."

Miss May read more of the email.

An emperor made this palace.

He made it for his wife.

He loved her very much.

He had more than 1,000 elephants.

These elephants
carried stones for
the building. 

## POP QUIZ

**What word describes the pool?**

ⓐ deep
ⓑ shiny

**KEY WORDS**

- pool
- shiny
- grass
- **grow** (grow-grew-grown)
- top
- cupcake

- listen for
- emperor
- **make** (make-made-made)
- more than
- elephant
- carry

Chingage

Miss May pointed to the palace.

"It is made of white marble."

"Is it the Tower of London?" Dan asked. 

"No," Beth said.

"London is rainy and cold.

This place is hot."

"It is very old," Miss May said.

"It is over 350 years old."

Miss May pointed to the picture.

"Do you see the jewels in the walls?"

The children nodded.

▲ Tower of London



- be made of
- marble
- London
- rainy
- cold (↔ hot)
- over
- jewel
- wall
- nod

"I know!"

Todd raised his hand.

"My dad went there.

It is called the Taj Mahal." **Aha!**

"Very good, Todd," Miss May said.

"Its name means 'jewel of the palace.'"

Dan raised his hand.

"Where is the Taj Mahal?"

"Good question, Dan,"

Miss May told him.

"I will read more from

your keypals."

▲ Taj Mahal

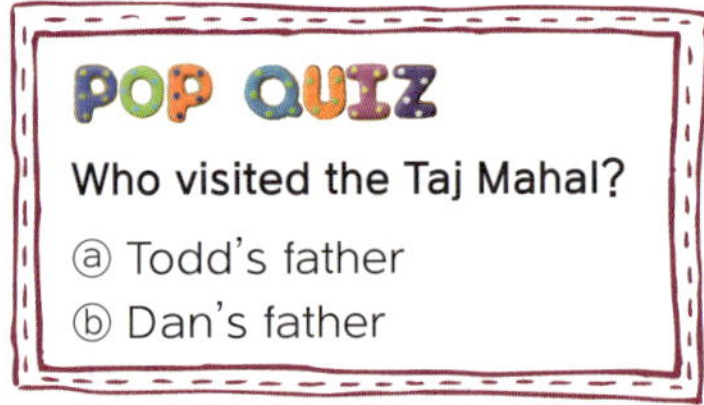


**KEY WORDS**

- raise one's hand
- **mean** (mean-meant-meant)
- question
- mountain
- jungle

Tigers live here.

Lions live here.

Monkeys live here, too.

We have tall mountains.

We have jungles.

We have rivers.

Our country is very big.

The children thought and thought.

"A map will help us."

Miss May tapped on the computer.

It showed a map.

The map showed a continent.

"That is Asia!" Dan shouted.

Next, the map showed India.

"India starts with the letter 'I,'" said Beth.

"The letter 'i' is a vowel.

That was a clue."

"India is hot. That was a clue," Todd said.

"You are right."

Miss May read more.



- **think** (think-thought-thought)
- help
- continent
- Asia
- shout
- India

Did you guess the Taj Mahal?
You are right.
It is in Agra, India.

Namaste,
Your keypals in India

"May we take a class trip there?" Beth asked.
"I like it."
Miss May laughed.
"Perhaps when you grow up, you can go,"
she told Beth.
"It is far away from us."

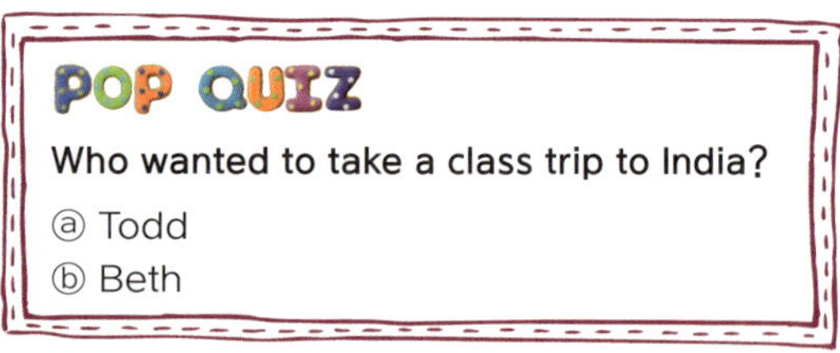


**KEY WORDS**

- Agra
- namaste
- take a class trip
- laugh
- perhaps
- grow up
- lucky

"Kass is lucky," said Dan.

"She visited Agra, India."

# Comprehension Quiz

**A** Circle all the words that describe the Taj Mahal.

white

old

pretty

leaning

**B** Mark T for true or F for false.

❶ The Ganges is a big palace in India.　T　F

❷ Kass sat on one side of the palace.　T　F

**C** Choose the best answer to the question.

Why did the emperor make the Taj Mahal?

a) because he loved his country

b) because he loved his wife

c) because he wanted to live in it

d) to give elephants work to do

# D Solve the crossword puzzle.



❺ the shape of the roof of the Taj Mahal



❶ The Taj Mahal is the p________ in Agra, India.

❷ the animal that brought stones

❸ The walls are made out of this.

❹ something in the walls of the Taj Mahal

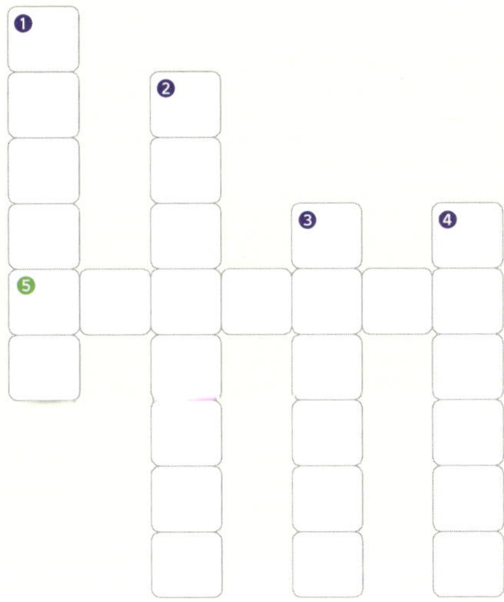

# Chapter Four

# Kel Is Hot and Cold

It was Wednesday.

Miss May talked to the children.

"We have an email from our keypals."

She tapped on the computer.

A picture showed Kel.

Kel wore the pink bow.

She sat in tall grass.

She sat in front of a big mountain.

Miss May asked, "Do you know where the mountain is?"

Dan pointed to the picture.

"It is right there!"

The children laughed.

**KEY WORDS**

- Wednesday
- talk to
- right there

Kel
F G H
J K L
N O P
S T X
V W X

"What country is this mountain in?" Miss May asked.

The children shook their heads.

They tapped their chins.

They thought hard.

"I see an elephant," Todd said.

"Yes. It has very big ears."

Miss May told them.

"I see a zebra." Beth pointed to it.

"There is a giraffe." Dan pointed to one.

"Kel is in Africa!"

Dan jumped up.

"You're right, Dan.

Now please sit down."

Miss May opened a map on the screen.

It showed the whole world.

"Africa is a big place."

"It has many countries,"

Beth said.

"I read that in a book."

"Yes, Beth," Miss May said.

"It has more than 55

countries."

She read the email.

▲ The African continent has many countries.

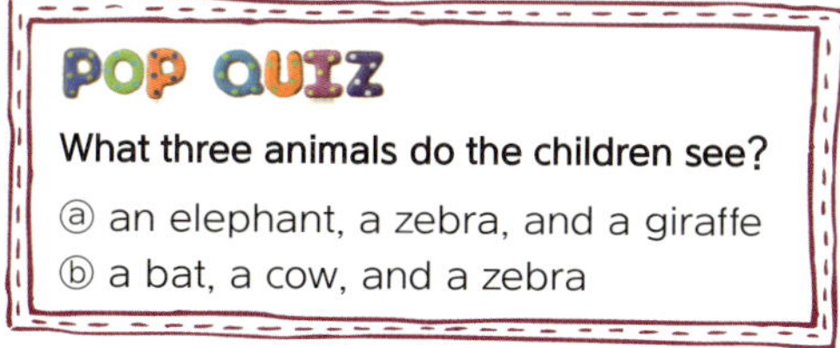


**KEY WORDS**

- shake one's head
  (shake-shook-shaken)
- chin

- hard (↔ soft)
- zebra
- giraffe

- Africa
- now
- the whole world

▲ Mount Kilimanjaro

Dear keypals,

We love Kel.

Thank you for sending her.

Our country has a big mountain.

It is called Mount Kilimanjaro. Aha!

Some people say the name means "large rock."

It is the tallest mountain in Africa. Aha!

Our country is a hot place.

But the mountain has snow all year long.

Can you guess where we live?

"We read a story about that mountain," said Todd.

He tried to remember.

He tapped his finger on his head.

"It looks hot.

But there is snow on top of the mountain."

Dan rubbed his arms.

"The mountain is cold."

"It has an ice cap," Miss May told him.

The ice cap never melts.

- Mount Kilimanjaro
- large
- rock
- tallest
- all year long
- try to + *Verb*
- remember
- on top of
- rub
- arm
- ice cap
- never
- melt

"Poor Kel," Beth said.

"I hope she has a coat."

"Her fur is her coat," Dan said.

"I think I know where Mount Kilimanjaro is!" Aha!

Todd raised his hand.

"It is in Tanzania."

**KEY WORDS**

- poor
- hope
- coat
- fur
- wonder
- find out
- soon

Miss May nodded.

"Very good, Todd.

The country is Tanzania,"

Miss May told the class.

"It is on the continent of Africa."

"I wonder who will send an email next," Beth said.

"We will find out soon," Miss May told her.

**A** Circle all the words related to Mount Kilimanjaro.

tall

rainy

snow

small

**B** Fill in each blank with the right word below.

| country | rock | snow | grass |
|---|---|---|---|

❶ Kel sat in tall ______________.

❷ The top of Mount Kilimanjaro is covered with ______________.

❸ Tanzania is in Africa. It is a ______________.

❹ The name "Kilimanjaro" means "big ______________."

 Choose the best answer to each question.

❶ Where is Kel?

    a) by a river                 b) in front of a mountain

    c) on a zebra               d) under a tree

❷ Why do people call the mountain Kilimanjaro?

    a) It is a pretty name.

    b) It is named after the person who found it.

    c) The mountain is big and the name means large rock.

    d) It is named after an animal that lives there.

❸ How did Beth know Africa has many countries?

    a) She read it in a book.

    b) She visited Africa with her mother.

    c) She counted the countries on the map.

    d) Dan told her.

**D** Mark T for true or F for false.

❶ In summer all the snow on Mount Kilimanjaro melts.    T  F

❷ Mount Kilimanjaro is the shortest mountain in Africa.    T  F

# Chapter Five

On Thursday a new picture came.

Kip sat in front of a mountain.

The mountain was a rich green.

It had old, white houses on it.

A big, gray rock rose behind the mountain.

**KEY WORDS**

- **Thursday**
- **come** (come-came-come)
- **rich**
- **rise** (rise-rose-risen)
- **behind**
- **board**

"I know that place!"

Dan jumped up.

He pointed at the board.

"Please sit down, Dan," Miss May said.

"Where is it?" Beth asked.

"I will give you the clues," Miss May said.

*Hello keypals,*

*We are in South America.*

*Our country is very long and thin.*

*It is next to the Pacific Ocean.*

*We raise llamas.* 

*We make things with llama fur.*

*It is a kind of wool.*

*Can you guess where Kip is?*

Miss May opened the map.
She pointed to South America.

▲ llama

### KEY WORDS

- South America
- thin
- next to
- the Pacific Ocean
- raise

- llama
- a kind of
- wool
- look for
- one time

Todd and Beth looked for a long, thin country.

They looked next to the ocean.

Dan looked at the picture with Kip.

"My dad went there one time.

His picture looks just like that."

▲ Machu Picchu

"Do you know the name of the place?" Miss May asked.

"That is Machu Picchu," Dan told the class. Aha!

Miss May nodded.

"Very good. Its name means 'old peak.'

Do you see the tall, gray rock?

That is the peak.

It is very high in the mountains.

It is almost 2,430 meters high," she said.

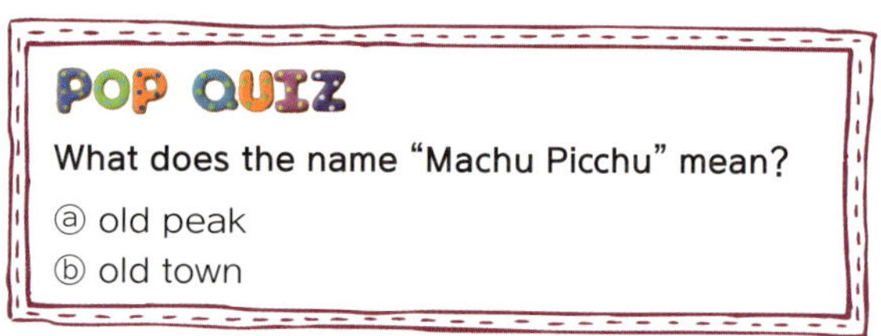


**KEY WORDS**

- Machu Picchu
- peak
- almost

Beth pointed to the map.

"This is the country of Peru."

"Yes, Beth," Miss
May said.

"Peru is part of
South America.
Long ago,
people lived there.
They were called
the Inca. **Aha!**
They built this city.
They built it with stone blocks."

"How long ago was it?" asked Dan.

"Almost 600 years ago," Miss May answered.

"That is very old!" Dan said.

"That is older than my grandfather!" **Aha!**

Miss May laughed.

"You are right.

The Inca made the stones fit together.

They fit them together very well.

That is why the buildings are still there.

In over 500 years they did not break down."

"Do the Inca still live there?" Dan asked.

Miss May said no.

"Not for a long time.

People found the city again in 1911."

She tapped the computer.

"I will read more of the email."


*We hope you like the picture.*

*We are happy to have Kip.*


*Adios,*

*Your keypals in Peru*

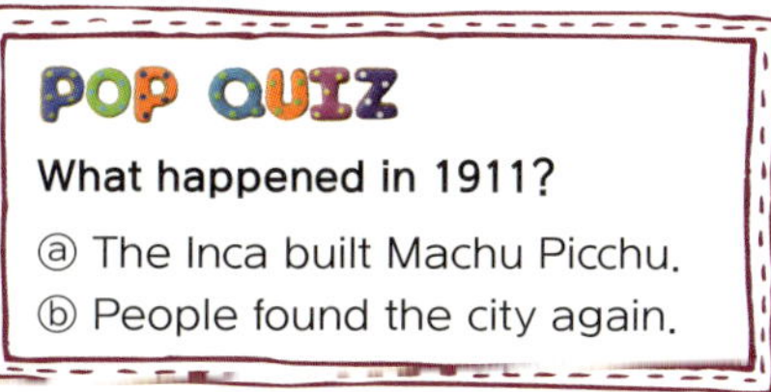


**KEY WORDS**

- How long ~?
- older
- fit
- still

- **break down** (break - broke - broken)
- for a long time
- be happy to + *Verb*
- adios

**A**  Who said what? Match each line with the right character.

**❶** 

**❷** 

**❸** 

a) "That is older than my grandfather!"

b) "People found the city again in 1911."

c) "This is the country of Peru."

**B**  Mark T for true or F for false.

**❶** The mountain has old, white houses on it.  `T` `F`

**❷** Machu Picchu is in Peru.  `T` `F`

**❸** The Inca left Machu Picchu a short time ago.  `T` `F`

**❹** The stones in the buildings fit together very well.  `T` `F`

C Choose the best answer to each question.

❶ When did people build Machu Picchu?

a) It was built about 50 years ago.

b) It was built about 100 years ago.

c) It was built about 600 years ago.

d) It was built about 1,000 years ago.

❷ In Peru, people make many things using this animal's fur. What is this animal?

a) horse

b) rabbit

c) llama

d) camel

❸ What is NOT mentioned about the mountain Kip sat in front of?

a) The mountain had a big, gray rock.

b) The mountain was a rich green.

c) The mountain had many flowers.

d) The mountain had old, white houses.

# Ken in the Sun

Now it was Friday.

"Did you get an email?" Dan asked.

"Did you get a picture?"

Miss May nodded yes.

"Our keypals sent an email.

They sent a picture of Ken."

The picture showed big, white sails.

The sails were beside the water.

"Those are big sails," Beth said.

Miss May nodded.

"It looks like sails.

I think it looks like shells."

**KEY WORDS**

- Friday
- **get** (get-got-gotten)
- sail
- beside
- shell

Beth tipped her head to the side.

She looked at the picture.

"Yes, it does look like shells." 

"But it is a building," Miss May told the children.

"It is a very big building."

"There is Ken in the picture!" Dan shouted.

"See? He is wearing his yellow tie."

"Ken looks small," Beth said.

"That is because the building is big."

Todd pointed to the picture.

"It looks hot," Dan said.

"Is Ken in Africa?"

"No, it is not Africa," Miss May said.

"Guess again."

"It is by the ocean."

Beth pointed to the water.

"Is Ken in Peru?"

"No, it is not Peru," Miss May told her.

"What do you think, Todd?"

"Will you please read the email?" he asked.

"The email will give us clues."

"Yes, I will read the email."

Miss May tapped on her computer.

Dear keypals,

Thank you for the gift.
We like Ken the koala bear.
There is a beautiful
building in the picture.
We went to see a dance
there.
We went to see a play there.
We went to hear music there.
Some people say our country is "down under."
That is because our country is near the bottom
of the world.
Do you know where we are?

**KEY WORDS**

- play
- down under
- near
- bottom
- Antarctica

- be full of
- Australia
- Sydney
- opera
- harbor

"I know!" Dan raised his hand.

"It is Antarctica."

"No," Todd told him.

"Antarctica is full of snow and ice."

"Maybe it is Australia," Dan said.

Beth clapped her hands.

"The Sydney Opera House is in Australia." 

"Ken is at Sydney Harbor," Todd said.

"The harbor is the water."

Miss May laughed.

"You are all very smart."

## POP QUIZ

**How did Todd know the picture wasn't taken in the South Pole?**

ⓐ He has known Antarctica has snow and ice.

ⓑ The keypals told him in the email.

▼ Sydney Opera House at Sydney Harbor

"People come from all over the world.

They want to see the Sydney Opera House,"

Miss May said.

"What do people do there?" Beth asked.

"They watch dances.

They see plays on the stage.

They listen to music."

Miss May told them more.

"In the summer there is a special holiday.

It is called Vivid Sydney. Aha!

The sails light up with art and pictures.

Now I have a surprise."

▲ Vivid Sydney

Miss May held a small box.

"It is from some of our keypals."

"Who sent it?" Todd asked.

"I will give you a clue.

The flag is green, white, and red."

"It is from Italy!" Beth smiled.

Miss May opened the box.

She took out a letter.


*Dear keypals,*


*We had fun with Koko.*

*We each wrote you a letter.*

*Here is a gift for you.*

*It is Italian candy.*

*Please enjoy it!*

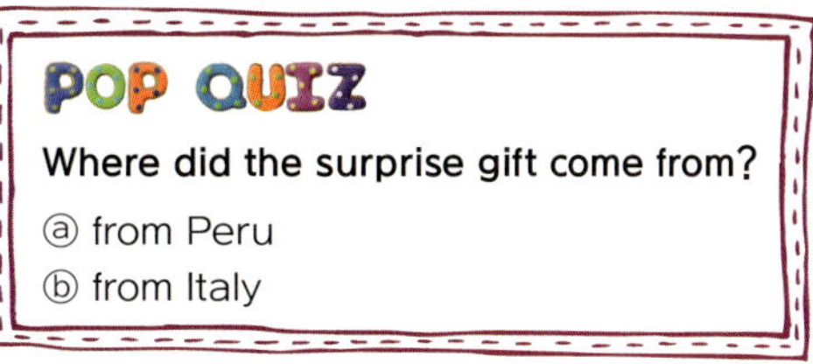


**KEY WORDS**

- **hold** (hold-held-held)
- **be from**
- **have fun**
- **write** (write-wrote-written)
- **Italian**
- **enjoy**

The children cheered.

Miss May got some candy, too.

Todd popped one in his mouth.

"I like sweets. Yum!"

"Our toy koala bears went around the world,"
Beth said.



- cheer
- pop one in one's mouth
- sweets
- yum
- make a friend
- term

"We made new friends," Dan said.

Todd smiled.

"I hope we can do this again."

"Yes," Miss May said.

"Next term we can have new keypals."

The children clapped their hands.

Miss May was very happy.

# Chapter Six

# Comprehension Quiz

**A** Circle the character which said each line.

❶ "Those are big sails."   **Dan / Beth / Todd**

❷ "There is Ken in the picture!"   **Dan / Beth / Todd**

❸ "Antarctica is full of snow and ice."   **Dan / Beth / Todd**

**B** Fill in each blank with the right word below.

| ocean | shells | art |
| --- | --- | --- |

❶ Miss May thought the sails looked like ____________.

❷ The Sydney Opera House is by the ____________.

❸ During a special summer holiday the sails light up with ____________ and pictures.

**C** Mark T for true or F for false.

❶ Antarctica is hot.   T  F

❷ The sails on the Sydney Opera House are very blue.   T  F

❸ People come from all over the world to see the Sydney Opera House.   T  F

 Choose the best answer to each question.

**❶** What do NOT people do at the Sydney Opera House?

a) People see dances.

b) People see plays.

c) People listen to music.

d) People cook food.

**❷** Why do some people say Australia is "down under?"

a) Because it has many caves.

b) Because it is close to the bottom of the world.

c) Because it is under the water.

d) Because it has special animals under the ground.

**❸** Where did the candy come from?

a) It came from Peru.

b) It came from Africa.

c) It came from Italy.

d) It came from India.

Fill in the blanks to review the story.

**Title:** The Secret Travels of __________ Bears

**Main Characters:** Miss __________, Dan, B__________, and __________

**Setting:** In the classroom

**Sequence:**

- In the beginning, Miss May sent the k________ b________ to boys and girls around the world. They sent the class emails and p________.

- First, Miss May and her students got an email from I________. In the picture, Koko was in front of the Leaning __________ of Pisa.

- After that, they got an email from I________. Kass was in front of the Taj __________ in the picture.

- Next, they got an email from T__________. In the picture, Kel was sitting in front of Mount K__________.

- Then they got an email from P__________. Kip was in Machu P__________ in the picture.

- Finally, they got an email from A__________. Ken was in front of the Sydney __________ House in the picture.

# Let's Think & Talk

**Think about the following questions and answer them freely.**

❶ Make a list of the names of the koala dolls, the places where they went and the features of those places.

❷ Which place do you want to go to the most among the places that the koala dolls visited? Tell us the reason why you want to go there.

❸ Except the places mentioned in the book, search for other places designated as World Heritage sites. Make a list these places and tell us where you want to go among them.

# Let's Review the Story

**Title:** The Secret Travels of Koala Bears

**Main Characters:** Miss May , Dan, Beth , and Todd

**Setting:** In the classroom

**Sequence:**

- In the beginning, Miss May sent the koala bears to boys and girls around the world. They sent the class emails and pictures .

- First, Miss May and her students got an email from Italy . In the picture, Koko was in front of the Leaning Tower of Pisa.

- After that, they got an email from India . Kass was in front of the Taj Mahal in the picture.

- Next, they got an email from Tanzania . In the picture, Kel was sitting in front of Mount Kilimanjaro .

- Then they got an email from Peru . Kip was in Machu Picchu in the picture.

- Finally, they got an email from Australia . Ken was in front of the Sydney Opera House in the picture.

# After-reading Test

- The Secret Travels of Koala Bears
- Level 1
- 18 Questions

(Vocabulary 5 / Reading Comprehension 10 /

Sentence Structure & Grammar 3)

1. Which is similar in meaning to the word "gift?"

   ① tower                  ② sweets

   ③ flag                   ④ present

2. Which of the following pairs has the wrong past tense form of the listed verb?

   ① put — put

   ② eat — ate

   ③ sit — sit

   ④ read — read

3. Which is a pair of words that are opposites?

   ① soft ↔ heavy

   ② cold ↔ hot

   ③ happy ↔ lucky

   ④ jewel ↔ sail

4. Each word is a specific example of the word listed on the right side.
   Which one is an incorrect example?

   ① cupcake → food

   ② jungle → place

   ③ shell → country

   ④ zebra → animal

5. Which is the correct word for the blank?

   > It is made __________ white marble.

   ① of                     ② but

   ③ off                    ④ than

6. What did Miss May ask the keypals to do when she sent the koala dolls
to them?
① feed the koala bears
② send an email
③ call on the telephone
④ do nothing

7. What shape is Italy?
① a boot
② a tower
③ a bell
④ a bow

8. The bell tower in Italy is part of what?
① a school
② a house
③ a church
④ an office

9. How can people go up the Leaning Tower of Pisa?
① They use an elevator.
② They use the 297 steps.
③ They use a ladder.
④ No one can go up the tower.

10. Which two things are true about the Taj Mahal?
① It has walls of white marble.
② It is over 350 years old.
③ It is 50 years old.
④ It is near the ocean.

11. Where is the Taj Mahal?
　① India
　② Italy
　③ Peru
　④ Africa


12. Why does Dan think Kel is in Africa?
　① He saw animals from Africa in the picture.
　② He saw a sign in the picture.
　③ Kel was holding a flag from Africa.
　④ He liked Africa.


13. Who lived in Machu Picchu long ago?
　① Americans
　② Incas
　③ Italians
　④ Indians


14. What is the name of the special summer festival held in Australia?
　① Vivid Sydney
　② Sydney Fun
　③ Opera Festival
　④ Melbourne Fever


15. Where did the surprise gift that Miss May's class got at the end come from?
　① from Peru
　② from Italy
　③ from Africa
　④ from India

※ Choose the wrong part of each sentence. (16~17)

16.
They will visited other countries.
　①　　②　　③　　④

17.
I think I know where is Mount Kilimanjaro!
　①　　②　　③　　　　④

18. Choose the correct words for the blank.

It ___________ like shells.

① do looks　　　　② do look
③ does look　　　　④ did looks

# Memo

# Memo 

# Memo

# Memo

**Suzanne Pitner**

Suzanne Pitner is a teacher and writer who has enjoyed visiting Alaska, exploring Rome, teaching in China, and is looking forward to more world travel. She has a Master's Degree in Education, and is a graduate of the Long Ridge Writer's Group. In addition to writing educational articles and books, she writes historical fiction and contemporary fiction for young adults using the pen name Suzanne Lilly.

# The Secret Travels of Koala Bears

Written by Suzanne Pitner
Illustrated by Gyeonga Jeong

First Published in October 2015

Editorial Manager: Juyon Choi
Editors: Kyunghee Jang, Jiyeong Park
Designers: Eunhee Lee, Elim
Cover Designer: Eunhee Lee

Published and distributed by

Darakwon Bldg., 64-1 Jandari-ro, Mapo-gu, Seoul, Korea 04031
Tel: 82-2-736-2031(ext. 250)      Fax: 82-2-732-2037
Homepage: www.ihappyhouse.co.kr
Publisher: Kyudo Chung



ISBN: 978-89-6653-208-7 18740 / 978-89-6653-156-1 18740(set)

[Components]
• 1 Audio CD (Recording Studio: Aram)
• Answer Keys & Korean Translation: Free download at www.ihappyhouse.co.kr